Tall Talk

Poems by Jill Eggleton
Illustrated by Philip Webb

CONTENTS

Rigby

The Juniper Tree

The gorillas came
out of the jungle,
beating their chests
with glee.
The gorillas came
out of the jungle,
and sat in our Juniper Tree!

A parrot came
out of the jungle,
as bold as bold
can be.
It chased
the **hairy** gorillas
away from our Juniper Tree!

2

3

The Peacock

"I am *very, very* handsome,"
the peacock said,
as he fanned out his tail,
and he fluffed up his head.
"I am *very, very* handsome . . .
oh, can't you see?"
And he strutted around
saying, "Look at me!"

"Yes, silly peacock,
look at you!
You're a handsome bird,
but a **show-off**, too!"

My Aunt

My aunt is outrageous —
a comic, a clown!
When she goes out,
she's the talk of the town!

Sometimes she wears
a furry old coat
with bunches of lace
puffed up at her throat.

Sometimes she wears
a patch on her eye
or a ring in her ear
like a pirate or spy!

Sometimes she wears
no shoes on her feet
and dances and prances
all over the street.

My aunt is outrageous —
a comic, a clown!
But everyone's happy
when she is in town!

Rastus

Rastus lives in a house
by the sea,
and he's as happy
as a man can be.

His shoes are tattered,
and his toes are bare,
and a spider made a web
in his tangled-up hair.

But he sings as he walks
with his little pet flea,
"I'm as happy
as a man can be!
I'm as happy
as a man can be!"

My Snake

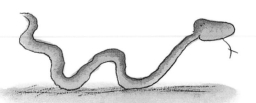

I left the snake cage open
and my snake, he slipped away.

He curled up
in a slipper,
just to sleep ther
for the day.

She put her slipper on
and she didn't see my snake!

It was my grandma's slipper, and she made a big mistake.

So she screamed,
and she screamed,
then she fainted on
the floor!
But my snake
doesn't bite,
so what's the fussing for?

11

My Friend Bert

My friend Bert,
who lives next door,
is really old,
about ninety-four.
His house is full
of marvelous things —
china dragons
with purple wings,
balls of glass
with silver inside,
nooks and crannies,
and places to hide.

"I was a sailor,"
Bert would say
"Then I gave
my sailing ship away,
for sailors must be
young, and free . . .
but I kept a treasure
chest for me."

And when I ask to
take a peep
at treasures from
the ocean deep,
Bert says that he
can't let me see,
for somehow he has
lost the key.

So . . .
down I sit
on the battered lid
and listen to
the things he did.

He was a sailor,
that's for sure.
Now he's my friend
who lives next door.

The Rainbow Man

The Rainbow Man is busy
with his rainbow color sack,
collecting different colors
  every day . . .
just in case the Color Robber
comes sneaking through the town
and snatches all the colors
zap away!

The Rainbow Man gets colors
for the flowers and the birds.
He has every kind of color
  in his sack.
And if the Color Robber
snatches colors from the town,
the Rainbow Man will **zap**
the colors back!

Poor Frog

I heard someone say
the other day
that my frog has
oogly eyes.
And skinny legs,
and feet they say, that are
a ridiculous shape and size.

I heard someone say
the other day,
that my frog has
slimy skin.
And a long, long tongue
and a big wide mouth
to keep that big tongue in!

I heard someone say
the other day,
that my frog has
an ugly head.

And my poor old frog,
I'm sure he heard,
he heard
what that someone said!

The Giant Jerome of Jo-joo

There once was a giant, Jerome of Jo-joo,
and it was amazing what he could do!
When he laughed, he cracked the houses in two!
That giant Jerome of Jo-joo!

He wore a big hat that fell over his eyes
and a bright red coat of **gi-normous** size,
and around his neck he wore polka dot ties!
That giant Jerome of Jo-joo!

That giant Jerome was a terrible tease,
he tickled the bees and the birds in the trees,
and **what a mess**, if he ever did sneeze!
That giant Jerome of Jo-joo!

His hair was yellow with streaks of green,
he had a big hole where a tooth had been,
but he never was scary, or nasty, or mean!
That giant Jerome of Jo-joo!

Rock King

An old goat perched
on the top of the rock,
where he thought
the world could see,
and he bleated loud,
and he bleated long,
"Everyone, listen to me!

"I'm the king of the rock!
I am brave! I am bold!
I'm the boss of the land
and the sea!
I'm the king of the rock!
I'm the king, I am!
No one is better than me!"

A bumblebee perched
on the head of the goat,
and he gave the goat a sting.
"Now tell me, tell me, tell me, Goat!
Tell me, who is king!"

Where Does a Laugh Come From?

Where does a laugh come from?
Is it deep inside my tum?
I can feel it bubbling there,
and I know it's going to come.

Then out and out
it **BUBBLES**,
like a fizzy soda pop,
and it keeps on bubbling, bubbling,
until something makes it stop!

It must go back inside me,
back deep inside my tum.
So I'll just have to wait
for another one to come!

Sammy Spats' Hats

Sammy Spats
wore fifteen hats —
he piled them on his head.
He wore them
everywhere he went.
"I love them," Sammy said.

One day
a rude and rowdy wind
came rushing, roaring by.
It snatched those hats
from Sammy Spats,
and spun them in the sky.

Now if one day,
when you are out,
and hats go flying by,
they're just the hats
of Sammy Spats —
so grab them from the sky.